£3

Motive Power Rev

GW00644811

BOOK OF
THE
THIRTY-THREE'S

BRITISH RAIL
CLASS 33's

Norman Preedy

PETER WATTS
Publishing

Published in Great Britain by
Peter Watts Publishing,
13-15 Stroud Road,
Gloucester, GL1 5AA.

ISBN 0 906025 53 2

First printed 1983
by
Gloster Graphics Ltd.

Typesetting by
Trio Graphics Ltd.

All photographs are by the author unless credited otherwise.

Nameplate of 33056

INTRODUCTION

The class 33 locomotives were built by the Birmingham Railway, Carriage and Wagon Co. Ltd. between the years of 1960 and 1962 and altogether 98 examples were constructed. They were, and still are, allocated to the Southern Region and initial duties included replacing steam traction prior to the East Kent electrification project and general freight/parcel duties. They became the workhouse of the Southern Region as steam disappeared altogether.

In 1967, when the London – Bournemouth electrification scheme became operative nineteen of the class were converted for push-pull operation over the non-electrified route between Bournemouth and Weymouth. These locomotives (classified 33/1's) were equipped to work in multiple with S.R. electric multiple units, 4-TC (class 491) stock and class 73 electro-diesels.

The class is divided into three sub-classes. The **33/0's** (63 in total) are the basic 'Crompton' and like the rest have electric train heating equipment. The **33/1's** (19 in total) are fitted with push-pull control gear and are nicknamed 'Bagpipes', whilst the **33/2's** (12 in total) are built to the narrower Hastings line gauge. Their nickname is 'Slim Jims'.

Four class members have been withdrawn to date, all through accident damage, these being D6502, D6576, 33036 and 33041. The rest are maintained exclusively on the Southern Region with Eastleigh Works responsible for all overhauls, although Slade Green Depot undertakes some work. The 'home' depots of Hither Green (HG) and Eastleigh (EH) do all routine servicing. Credit must go to the maintenance staff of these depots as over the years the reliability and availability has remained at a very good level.

Today 'Cromptons' have regular turns around the country and can be seen as far afield as Preston, Fishguard Harbour, Plymouth and Margate at the head of all types of traffic.

The future looks assured and the modern enthusiast can look forward to seeing these sturdy Bo-Bo locomotives working hard into the 1990's.

33001 (D6500)   21st August 1979   Woking

(John Augustson)

33002 (D6501)   4th June 1980   Banbury

33003 (D6503) 16th April 1974 Reading General

33004 (D6504) 14th August 1974 Fairwood Junction, Westbury

33005 (D6505) 24th March 1982 Cardiff Central
(Ray Hinton)

33006 (D6506) 19th June 1982 Cheltenham

33007 (D6507) 18th August 1982 Birmingham New Street
(Ray Hinton)

EASTLEIGH
33008 (D6508) 9th April 1983 Hereford

33009 (D6509)   11th December 1974   Exeter St. Davids

33010 (D6510)   29th January 1983   Bristol Bath Road

33011 (D6512)   12th February 1983   Bristol Temple Meads

33012 (D6515)   18th September 1982   Bristol Temple Meads

33013 (D6518)   19th January 1983   Bristol Temple Meads

(John Chalcraft)

33014 (D6522)   5th March 1983   Bristol Temple Meads

33015 (D6523)   29th May 1980   **Westbury**
                                                 (John Chalcraft)

                                                 (Ray Hinton)
33016 (D6524)   19th August 1980   **Portsmouth Harbour**

33017 (D6526)   12th February 1983   Cardiff Central

33018 (D6530)   15th March 1983   Barnwood, Gloucester

33019 (D6534)   8th April 1980   Wolverhampton

(Ray Hinton)

33020 (D6537)   19th August 1980   Portsmouth Harbour

33021 (D6539)   30th July 1975   Westbury

33022 (D6540)   23rd May 1976   Exeter St. Davids

33023 (D6541)　　　　　6th March 1975　　　　　Westbury

(Ray Hinton)

33024 (D6542)　　　　　23rd May 1981　　　　Bristol Temple Meads

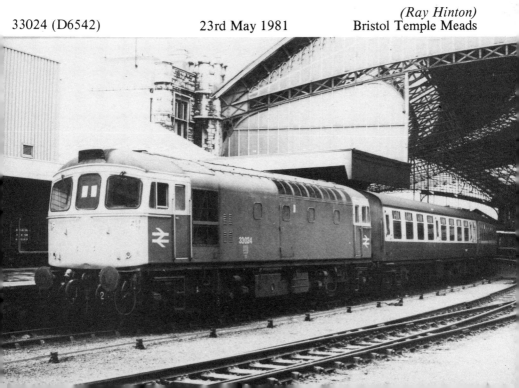

33025 (D6543)　　　　　19th February 1983　　　　Bristol Bath Road
SULTAN

33026 (D6544)　　　　　1st March 1976　　　　Exeter St. Davids

33027 (D6545)   23rd April 1983   Cardiff Central

EARL MOUNTBATTEN OF BURMA

33028 (D6546)   6th June 1983   Barnwood, Gloucester

33029 (D6547)   29th January 1983   Bristol Bath Road
(Ray Hinton)

33030 (D6548)   9th July 1974   Reading General

33031 (D6549)   24th March 1979   Exeter Central

(Ray Hinton)
33032 (D6550)   19th August 1980   Portsmouth Harbour

33033 (D6551)   13th November 1982   Hereford

33034 (D6552)   9th July 1983   *(Ray Hinton)*
Salisbury

33035 (D6553) 16th July 1983 Exeter St. Davids

33036 (D6554) 19th April 1977 (Eric Bullen) Eastleigh Works

33037 (D6555)   25th March 1978   Hither Green Depot

(John Chalcraft)
33038 (D6556)   28th October 1978   Hither Green Depot

33039 (D6557) 15th January 1983 Cardiff Central

33040 (D6558) 11th May 1974 March

33041 (D6559)   8th March 1975   Reading General
(Eric Bullen)

33042 (D6560)   26th March 1983   Bristol Bath Road

33043 (D6561)   29th January 1983   Bristol Temple Meads
(Ray Hinton)

33044 (D6562)   8th January 1983   Bristol Temple Meads

33045 (D6563)   4th September 1982   Bristol Temple Meads

(John Augustson)

33046 (D6564)   14th July 1979   Hither Green Depot

33047 (D6565)   28th October 1978   **Hither Green Depot**
(John Chalcraft)

33048 (D6566)   28th May 1983   **Bristol Bath Road**

A scene soon to be changed forever with the introduction of multi-aspect signals between Westbury and Newton Abbot. 33057 trundles over the level crossing at the east end of Exeter St. Davids with the 16.45 from Barnstaple on 16th July 1983.

33049 (D6567)   6th April 1983   Bristol Temple Meads
(Ray Hinton)

33050 (D6568)   27th February 1982   Dover

33051 (D6569)   31st May 1983   Bristol Bath Road

ASHFORD
33052 (D6570)   17th September 1983   Bristol Bath Road

33053 (D6571)   25th September 1982   Bristol Temple Meads

(John Augustson)

33054 (D6572)   21st August 1979   London Bridge

33055 (D6573)   22nd February 1975   West Ealing

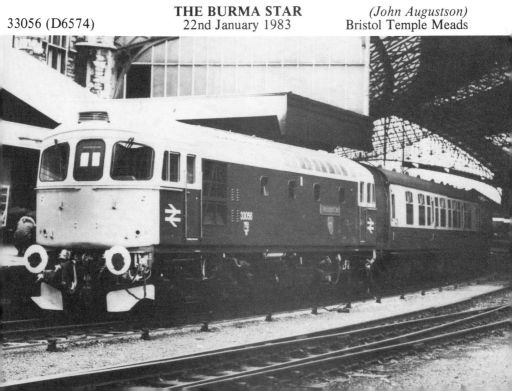

33056 (D6574)

THE BURMA STAR
22nd January 1983

(John Augustson)
Bristol Temple Meads

33057 (D6575)   9th July 1983   Bristol Temple Meads

33058 (D6577)   28th May 1983   Bristol Bath Road

33059 (D6578)   5th February 1983   Bristol Bath Road

                                          (Ray Hinton)
33060 (D6579)   1st May 1982   Bristol Temple Meads

33061 (D6581) 9th June 1974 Gloucester Eastgate

33062 (D6582) 19th February 1983 Bristol Temple Meads

33063 (D6583)   7th August 1982   Bristol Bath Road

33064 (D6584)   12th July 1983   Gloucester

33065 (D6585)   25th March 1978   Hither Green Depot

33101 (D6511)   28th February 1981   Bristol Bath Road

33102 (D6513) 27th July 1974 Eastleigh
(Derek Hawkins)

33103 (D6514) 24th December 1982 Birmingham New Street

33104 (D6516)   29th January 1983   Bristol Temple Meads
(Ray Hinton)

33105 (D6517)   26th March 1983   Bristol Temple Meads

33106 (D6519)   24th April 1976   Reading General

(Eric Bullen)

33107 (D6520)   30th April 1981   Bournemouth

| 33108 (D6521) | 27th July 1974 | Eastleigh |
| | | *(Derek Hawkins)* |

| 33109 (D6525) | 27th July 1975 | Exeter St. Davids |

33110 (D6527) 7th August 1982 Birmingham New Street
(Ray Hinton)

(Eric Bullen)

33111 (D6528) 19th April 1977 Eastleigh

33112 (D6529)　　　　9th July 1983　　　　Salisbury
(Ray Hinton)

(P. White)
33113 (D6531)　　　　2nd April 1983　　　　Weymouth

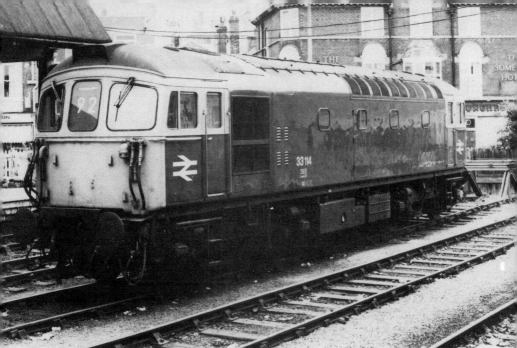

33114 (D6532)   5th June 1976   Weymouth

33115 (D6533)   5th June 1976   Weymouth Quay

33116 (D6535)   31st March 1979   Eastleigh Depot
(John Augustson)

33117 (D6536)   5th June 1976   Weymouth

33118 (D6538)   15th July 1978   Bincombe Tunnel, Weymouth

(both John Chalcraft)

33119 (D6580)   5th March 1983   Bristol Bath Road

33201 (D6586)   15th May 1982   Hither Green Depot
(John Augustson)

(Colin Marsden)
33202 (D6587)   9th October 1982   Hither Green Depot

33203 (D6588)   17th March 1979   Hither Green Depot
                                                        (Eric Bullen)

33204 (D6589)   28th May 1982   *(John Augustson)*
                                                     Salisbury

33205 (D6590)   9th October 1982   Hither Green Depot
(Colin Marsden)

(John Augustson)

33206 (D6591)   1st September 1979   Hither Green Depot

33207 (D6592)   15th August 1976   Reading General

33208 (D6593)   25th June 1983   Bristol Temple Meads

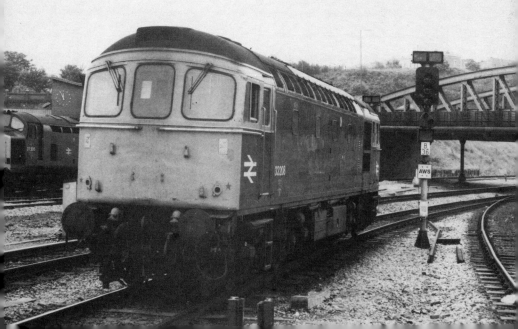

33209 (D6594)   25th June 1983   Bristol Temple Meads

33210 (D6595)   25th March 1978   Hither Green Depot

33211 (D6596)   25th July 1974   Hither Green Depot
(Derek Hawkins)

(John Chalcraft)
33212 (D6597)   28th October 1978   Hither Green Depot

–	(D6502)	March 1960	Weal[d]

(Derek Cross)

–	(D6576)	8th August 1964	Salisbur[y]

(John Faulkner)

Introduced: 1960-1962
Built: Birmingham Railway Carriage and Wagon Company
Wheel arrangement: Bo-Bo
Engine: Sulzer 8 cylinder 8LDA28
b.h.p.: 1550 at 750 r.p.m.
Transmission: four Crompton Parkinson nose suspended, axle hung C171C2 traction motors.
Maximum tractive effort: 45,000 lb.
Maximum Speed: 85 m.p.h.
Axle loading limit: 19½ tons (except 33/1-19¾ tons)
Weight in working order: 78 tons (except 33/1 - 79 tons)
Height: 12′ 8″
Width: 9′ 3″ (except 33/2 – 8′ 8″)
Length: 50′ 9″
Route availability: 6
Train heating: electric
Multiple Working Type: blue star

This book forms part of the 'Motive Power Review' library, a series which aims to record pictorially individual locomotives within their British Rail classes.

Titles published so far include:-

Book of the Westerns
Book of the Fifties
Book of the Seventy-Sixes
Book of the Deltics
Book of the Peaks I (class 44's)
Book of the Peaks II (class 46's)
Book of the Peaks III (class 45/0's)
Book of the Forties

Please send to the publisher for a complete list of current titles.

(Front Cover Photograph) 'Double Stamps to Brighton' - Class 33's no's 33042 + 33060 bask in the sun at Exeter St. Davids on 16th July 1983, awaiting the 'off' and following stiff climb to Exeter Central with the 10.50 Penzanze to Brighton service.

Powering past Fairwood Junction, Westbury on 20th July 1974 is 33009 at the head of empty hoppers bound for Whatley Stone Quarry.